# Helping Through Heartache

### An Easy Guide to Supporting Anyone Who Is Grieving

## Sheila Hoover

*To everyone with a broken heart.*

# Contents

# Introduction

People who are grieving need support. No one can pull through the devastating loss of a loved one without help from the people around them. Unfortunately, most of us are not taught how to support someone who is grieving and we often feel anxious in the presence of someone who is expressing intense emotions. This is understandable. No one likes to think about death and loss. Grieving people are a reminder of our own mortality and the grief we will likely face at some point in our lives (hopefully far in the future).

There are those rare individuals who seem to intuitively know just the right thing to say and do for a grieving person. But most of us have a much harder time. We worry that we will say or do the "wrong" thing and upset the grieving person even more. Fortunately, help is here in the form of this book!

This book will quickly teach you everything you need to know about how to support a grieving person, including:

- What is the "right" thing to say?
- What is the best way to help?
- How can I be supportive without being overbearing?
- Should I just give the person some space?

*Helping Through Heartache: An Easy Guide to Supporting Anyone Who is Grieving* contains dozens of practical, concise dos and don'ts for supporting someone who is grieving, whether they are a family member, friend, neighbor, coworker, or acquaintance. Using illustrations featuring the lovable Sad Cat (who represents the grieving person) and their cat friends, this book is actually fun to read!

Each page offers a different quick tip and amusing illustration. Although some of the suggestions may seem common sense, most Sad Cats have experienced difficult input from the most well-intended people. Every scenario in this book (the wonderful and the difficult) has happened to me or one of my Sad Cat friends.

You can use the table of contents to find the topic that speaks to you, you can open the book to any page, or you can read the book from cover to cover. The tips are intended to be read in any order you like.

At the core of all these tips is being sensitive to a very traumatized person, being gentle with them, being present, respecting their boundaries, and holding love and kindness in the face of their grief.

I felt moved to write this book after my husband passed away. I naively thought that passage in my life would be the time when everyone rallied around me with kindness, gentleness, and compassion. Instead, I got a confusing mashup of reactions: some people were wonderfully supportive, some tiptoed around me, fearing they'd inadvertently make me cry, some railroaded me with what *they* thought I needed, and some literally ran away from me as if I were the Grim Reaper. Over the years, I've heard similar reports from other Sad Cats.

I kept thinking, "There needs to be a simple handbook to teach people what to do." So I wrote this handbook. Most grief resources focus on the bereaved. This book was written for those who are *helping* the bereaved. The purpose of this book is to help people help a Sad Cat—to guide those who are afraid to step in, along with those who have a tendency to step in a little too far.

Traditionally, grief resources (such as hospice support groups) focus on people considered "elderly" whose loved ones have passed away after living long, full lives. This book was written to include a wide range of ages, including widows and widowers with young children. Death can be particularly upsetting when someone young passes away, or if a death is unexpected, traumatic, or by suicide. Sadly, these kinds of deaths are those that many people have the most trouble with because they are an unwelcome reminder that any of us could go at any time. I noticed that people were more comfortable extending condolences when my 93-year-old mother passed away than when my husband died unexpectedly, because her death felt more "natural" and therefore somehow more "acceptable."

All Sad Cats, no matter how their loved one died, need support and tender loving care.

It's important to appreciate that every Sad Cat is unique. Some of the recommendations in this book may not resonate with your Sad Cat. The important thing is that you try—do your best and take your cues from your Sad Cat, whether they are a close friend, family member, coworker, or acquaintance.

It's okay if you mess up and say or do the "wrong" thing! I still mess up when talking to other Sad Cats. Sad Cats tend to be very forgiving—they can tell when your heart is in the right place. It can take courage to hang in there with a Sad Cat even when things feel uncomfortable. And, honestly, death, dying, loss, and grief are always uncomfortable.

When reading this book, it's important to keep in mind how close you are to the Sad Cat. Some tips are more appropriate for those within the Sad Cat's inner circle of relationships and might come off as inappropriate if you don't know the Sad Cat very well. On the other hand, when someone loses a loved one, they often find that the people in their inner and outer circles change. Sometimes people who they thought would be there for them will disappear, and sometimes acquaintances step in and become very close friends.

Supporting a Sad Cat can be a gift—to the Sad Cat, of course, but also to yourself. If you can hang in there with a Sad Cat, you will have someone who will stand by you as you weather your own storms in life. What is more precious than that?

Over time, you may discover that your Sad Cat has a depth of character marked by resilience, strength, compassion, and wisdom. Sad Cats can be the most loving people you will ever encounter, often with a brilliantly dark sense of humor. Supporting a Sad Cat can teach you something beautiful about kindness and compassion in the midst of devastating heartbreak, which you will need yourself someday—we all will.

# Understanding
# a Sad Cat

# Appreciate How Painful Loss Is

When interacting with a Sad Cat, it can be helpful to appreciate these things:

- Sad Cats often feel like they have been blasted into another dimension—into an alternate reality where their world looks the same but feels completely foreign and unfamiliar.

- Sad Cats have experienced a trauma and may be in shock for a long time. This often comes with a range of symptoms, including brain fog, anxiety, loss of appetite, insomnia, etc.

- Grieving takes a lot of energy and Sad Cats are often extremely fatigued.

- Grief is not linear and can last for years. It comes in waves and phases over time. These waves of intense emotion can come out of nowhere, when a Sad Cat least expects them.

- If you have never experienced profound loss yourself, it can be helpful to keep in mind that no matter how intense you imagine a Sad Cat's pain to be, it's likely exponentially, infinitely worse, and therefore calls for as much kindness and compassion as you can offer.

best books on grief

top grief
websites

what is secondary loss?

being widowed

TED Talks
on grief

losing a child

# Do Some Research on Grief

A good starting point when supporting a Sad Cat is to educate yourself about grief. There are many books, blogs, videos, podcasts, articles, and other resources about grief.

A thoughtful gesture you could make is to send the Sad Cat a couple of books on grief, saying, "I did some research on which grief books people seemed to find the most helpful and I hope these are helpful to you." Then add something like, "I'm thinking of you and sending you love during this difficult time."

Be mindful not to come off as a grief expert who knows more than the Sad Cat, because *they* are living it. When talking about what you learned you could frame it as, "I was reading about grief and wanted to see if something I learned resonated with your experience."

# Understand that Every
# Sad Cat Grieves Differently

Every Sad Cat will deal with grief in their own unique way. Some Sad Cats may collapse and not be able to get out of bed. Some may become extremely productive. Some Sad Cats may drink a lot of alcohol. Some may get really into exercise. Some will over-eat and some will under-eat. Some will do all of the above, depending on the day.

Some Sad Cats are very public with their grief in an attempt to help others understand what they are going through (some may even start a blog or post about their pain on social media). Others are more private.

It's important not to judge a Sad Cat's grief expressions or coping strategies. There is no "right" way to cope with the loss of a loved one. There is no road map and there are no rules. The best thing you can do is meet your Sad Cat wherever they are with love and kindness.

# Understand that Asking "How Are You?" Is Tricky

We often ask, "How are you?" without giving it much thought. But that can be a loaded question for Sad Cats because few people can handle the real answer. It would be so much easier if our society had an expression that communicated "I wish you well" that didn't require a response.

Some Sad Cats are really open about the depth of their pain no matter who they're talking to. But for Sad Cats who are more reserved about sharing their feelings, the question "How are you?" presents them with the daunting task of sorting out what, exactly, to say—and whether the person can handle their response. This can be an exhausting and extremely painful learning process for a Sad Cat, always wondering "how much realness can they handle?"

So, depending on the situation, instead of asking, "How are you?" you could say:

- "I've been thinking about you."
- "It's nice to see you."

# Don't Treat Sad Cats
# Like Superheroes

Some people express profound admiration of a Sad Cat's ability to keep going, almost as if it were the result of superhuman strength. This can actually come across as insincere (or a projection of the person's own fear of loss) because Sad Cats don't have a choice about whether to keep going. Sad Cats don't have any more strength than anyone else; their strength is just being tested in a way that others may not have experienced.

That said, some Sad Cats find it encouraging when someone tells them sincerely "you are very strong." It's okay to test the waters and see how your Sad Cat responds.

life purpose
self-confidence
health
job / career
stability
hopes & dreams
identity
income
relationships

# Appreciate the Pain
## of "Secondary Losses"

Something that often takes Sad Cats by awful, painful surprise is *secondary loss*. Sad Cats not only lose their loved one, they often lose so much more, such as their *identity* (in relation to the deceased, such as a being spouse or a parent), *relationships* (when friends and relatives stop checking in because the sadness makes them too uncomfortable), *jobs and career* (if the Sad Cat had to stay home to take care of a loved one), *income* (if the household is down one income), their *health* (from the profound stress), *and so much more.*

Understanding that the Sad Cat is grieving all of this *on top of* the devastating grief of losing their loved one may help others better appreciate the magnitude of a Sad Cat's pain and help them treat the Sad Cat with greater sensitivity and compassion.

# Don't Assume a Sad Cat Is Doing Great

S ad Cats become masters of putting on a good front even when they are profoundly grieving on the inside. It's important not to presume a Sad Cat has moved on from their grief because they appear to be doing well. Sometimes Sad Cats are admonished for not "grieving enough." Keep in mind that just because you don't see outward evidence of a Sad Cat's grief, or if you see them laughing and having fun, it doesn't mean they're not grieving—they are most likely experiencing a tidal wave of grief in private, at home, in quiet moments.

Also, some Sad Cats are comfortable expressing grief in front of people and some are not. It may depend on your relationship to the Sad Cat. If you are someone who has regularly leaned on the Sad Cat for emotional support, they may not see you as someone who can provide emotional support to them.

# Don't Rush a Sad Cat

People often have opinions about when a Sad Cat should do certain things, such as give away their loved one's belongings, stop wearing a wedding ring, put away photos of their loved one, and so on. It's important to let the Sad Cat do things in their own time and not pressure them because *you* feel it's time. It can take years for a Sad Cat to deal with certain things and that's okay. Allow them the space to handle things as they are ready.

# Getting Ready
# To Help

I'm getting on
the next plane
there!

↗

Feels like they are a
friendship fail if they
don't show up right
away.

↗

Wants friend to come after the chaos
of the early days settles down and they
really need some company.

# Let Go of What You Think Help Looks Like

It's important to understand that what a Sad Cat actually needs might be very different to what *you* think they need. You may have a very definite idea of what you *should* or *want* to do to help, and it can be difficult to let go of those ideas.

When supporting a Sad Cat, it's very important to set aside your ideas of how things should be or what should happen, and defer to the Sad Cat's wishes. It's important to let go of your own point of view and listen to whatever the Sad Cat is telling you they need (or don't need).

# Don't Require Anything Extra of the Sad Cat

Sometimes people want to be helpful but unintentionally create more stress for a Sad Cat. If you want to do something helpful, think about whether it would require any effort on the part of the Sad Cat, and whether that effort would be too much of a burden for them. If so, rethink your offer so that it doesn't require too much of your Sad Cat's energy.

# Always Ask First, and Respect Their Answer

In general, it's always better to ask before doing something you think is helpful. If you offer to help and can't get a clear yes or no, it may be because the Sad Cat is in shock and can't process your request in that moment. Use your best, most sensitive judgment—if the task must be done right away, it may be best to just do it. If it's not that urgent, it may be best to wait until the Sad Cat can weigh in more definitively.

Really listen to what the Sad Cat is telling you. If a Sad Cat says no to your offer, respect that. If they say "I'll let you know," that means *no* (at least until they get back to you). Don't keep asking them until you get the answer *you* want.

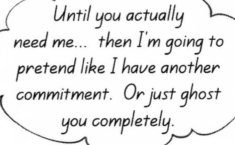

# Be Real About What You're Actually Up For

Sometimes people promise things they can't actually do. This usually happens when they get nervous or anxious during an emotional moment and say to a Sad Cat, "let me know if you need *anything*—I'm here for you if you need *anything at all!*" Try not to do this unless you actually mean it as it can lead to false expectations.

It's very painful when a Sad Cat musters all their courage in a moment of real need and calls someone who has offered to help, only to have the person casually tell them no, or not respond at all. If you tell a Sad Cat that you will be there for them, be sure that you mean it.

# Don't Expect
# Anything in Return

If you do something helpful for a Sad Cat, especially soon after their loved one dies, don't expect them to acknowledge it. Even if your loved one is typically very thoughtful about sending thank-you notes, understand that these are not normal circumstances for them. Know in your heart that you did a good deed to help them and let that be enough.

If you feel strongly that your Sad Cat needs to express some form of gratitude for a kindness, offer to send out thank-you notes yourself. If the Sad Cat declines your offer, respect that and then let it go.

# Be Careful About Cleaning

Many people think that cleaning a Sad Cat's house is always helpful. It may not be! What looks like garbage to you may be precious to the Sad Cat. A crumpled tissue might be the last tissue that held the tears of their loved one before they died. A used paper coffee cup might be the last thing their loved one drank from.

*Never do the laundry* unless you are absolutely sure it's okay. Sad Cats may feel a connection to their loved one in the scent of their clothes. Some Sad Cats like to hug their loved one's clothes. It can be devastating if a well-intentioned person does the laundry and erases the smell of their loved one from their life.

Likewise, never pack up a loved one's clothes or give them away until the Sad Cat signals it's okay to do so. Clothing can hold many precious memories, as Sad Cats can picture their loved one wearing each piece of clothing and remember times when they were together. It can take a long time for a Sad Cat to deal with their loved one's things, and that's okay. Let them do everything on their timeline.

# Be Respectful of Boundaries in the Sad Cat's Home

When a Sad Cat's loved one dies, their home can suddenly become filled with people. Boundaries and privacy go right out the window. Obviously, Sad Cats haven't prepared their home for visitors, yet all of a sudden, everyone is in their space.

Be considerate of how this would feel, and how having extra people in their house could add another layer of stress on top of their trauma. Be respectful of the Sad Cat's environment and conduct yourself so your presence causes the least stress and disturbance possible.

# Specific Ways
# To Help

# Propose Specific Tasks

People often say to a Sad Cat, "Let me know if you need anything" and leave it at that. Sad Cats, especially in the initial days or weeks after their person dies, may not know what they need because they are in shock or the deep throes of grief. It may also be difficult for a Sad Cat to be vulnerable and ask for help.

Make specific suggestions:

- "Can I come over and do the dishes?"
- "Can I come over with snacks and watch a movie with you?"
- "Can I babysit so you can take a shower?"

Think about what gaps are left by the person who died—were they responsible for car maintenance? If so, offer to check the Sad Cat's tires or take the car in for an oil change. Did they do the gardening? Offer to weed and water the garden.

# Give Restaurant or Grocery Delivery Gift Cards

In the early days after someone dies, people often drop off food or set up a meal train. This is a very kind gesture and may be very welcome, but Sad Cats may end up throwing food away if too much piles up and they are too overwhelmed to pack it and put it in the freezer. It's also common for Sad Cats to lose their appetite.

An alternative is to give gift cards to their favorite restaurants or grocery and meal delivery services. If a Sad Cat has children, it can be especially helpful to be able to grab a gift card and make dinner happen without much effort.

Feeling like they're doing the right thing by giving the Sad Cat some space.

*Bootsie keeps asking me how you're doing.*

Feeling like they're doing the right thing by telling the Sad Cat that people are concerned about them.

Wondering why everyone has disappeared and wishing they would get in touch.

# Check in with Sad Cats

Many people feel like the kindest thing to do is give the Sad Cat space and not bother them. This depends on your relationship to the Sad Cat. Are you in their innermost circle of relationships? If so, giving space might feel to the Sad Cat like you're avoiding them. If you're not in their inner circle, giving space may be the best thing to do, especially in the early days after the death. However, over time, it's good to check in.

It's painful for a Sad Cat to feel like people have dropped out of their lives, and then have someone tell them "so-and-so was asking how you are," instead of asking them directly. This reinforces the Sad Cat's feeling of disconnection. Generally speaking, Sad Cats would rather you reach out. When reaching out you could simply say, "Please don't feel any pressure to get back to me right away, I just wanted to let you know I'm thinking of you."

1.
Sad Cat
very sad

2.
Friend sends
a text

Thinking about you
today and wishing
you well.

3.
Sad Cat feels
a little better

# Make Small Gestures

The power of small gestures, such as sending a random text, can't be overstated. What you say in the text depends on your relationship to the Sad Cat, but you could write something simple like, "I've been thinking about you and wanted to say hi. No pressure to respond, I just wanted to check in."

Another gesture (again, depending on your relationship to the Sad Cat) is to send a postcard in the mail every so often that says, "Thinking of you and wishing you well" or "Thinking of you and sending love." It's not so much what you say but the gesture that's important.

Getting a friendly text or card in a difficult moment may help your Sad Cat more than you might imagine.

# Encourage Grief Breathers

Encouraging the Sad Cat to take a breather and do something enjoyable or rejuvenating requires sensitivity because, particularly in the early days, weeks, and even months, their grief can be all-consuming and they may not have the energy for anything else. Providing a Sad Cat with some relief from their grief can be a great help but it's important to find out what is in their comfort zone.

Ask your Sad Cat what they might find enjoyable (or, at least, not stressful). Would they like a massage? Do they want you to come over, drink wine, and watch TV with them? For how long do they want company? Are they tired of being stuck in the house with only their kids to talk to and would like to go out and spend time with another adult?

It's important to appreciate that some Sad Cats feel guilty about having a good time because they feel like it's disrespectful to their loved one's memory. You could (very) gently suggest that it might be good self-care to put their grief on the shelf for a couple of hours, just to give their hearts a little breather.

# Set Up a Standing Occasion

Having ongoing, regular connections with people can be helpful to Sad Cats, with the caveat that they can cancel if they wish, with no hard feelings. Depending on how close you are to the Sad Cat, you could propose going to their place every week and doing something enjoyable or helping the Sad Cat with housework or other specific tasks—whatever the Sad Cat wants. Make a specific suggestion and see what works for the Sad Cat.

no biggie

devastated & lonely

# Don't Casually Cancel a Social Occasion with a Sad Cat

Sad Cats, particularly those who have lost a partner, can be quite lonely. The promise of a social occasion with a friend can be precious—something they are really looking forward to. If you cancel on a Sad Cat, the Sad Cat may end up sitting home alone feeling even more lonely and isolated. Try not to cancel on a Sad Cat unless you really must, and then be prepared to reschedule right away for another day.

# Offer to Accompany
# Sad Cats to Appointments

For many Sad Cats, certain kinds of appointments can be upsetting. Going to a doctor's office or the hospital could be really difficult because it may be where they brought their loved one for appointments, or even where their loved one died. It may be very helpful for a Sad Cat to have some company for these appointments. (Note: don't offer this if going to doctor's offices or hospitals makes you nervous!)

A seemingly simple appointment, such as going to the social security office or to the bank, can also be very triggering because the Sad Cat must present the death certificate and explain that their loved one is deceased in order to complete transactions. If it seems appropriate, you could offer to go along and help them navigate any decisions, or just provide a reassuring presence.

Bonus points: If your Sad Cat lives alone, offer to help with follow-up care after a doctor's appointment. For example, if they need to change a bandage in a place they can't reach on their own, or if they can't drive you could offer to get groceries or run other errands for them.

# Offer to Be an SOS Person

An SOS person is someone who is willing to be available 24/7 if a Sad Cat needs help or just to talk to someone, even if it's in the middle of the night. In reality, most Sad Cats would never take someone up on it and actually call them in the middle of the night, but it gives the Sad Cat a sense of security knowing that there's someone they can call for help.

It's important to really commit to this if you offer it because it may turn out that the one night you turn off your phone is the night they need you.

# Remember the Sad Cat's Birthday

The first birthday without a loved one can be particularly brutal for some Sad Cats. It is a real kindness to offer to spend time with them that day. Prepare some ideas ahead of time and ask the Sad Cat if they would like to do any of them (rather than having them come up with ideas). You might suggest something as simple as going out for coffee or bringing them flowers. Tell them you don't mind if they are sad because you understand that it's a hard day.

# 1.
## Valentine's Day – Sad Cat very sad

"Thinking of you and sending love."

# 2.
## Friend sends valentine

Extra points for getting a card ahead of time and putting a reminder on the calendar to mail it.

# 3.
## Sad Cat feels a little better

# Send a Card on Holidays

Sad Cats are generally very appreciative when people acknowledge that holidays are difficult. Sad Cats aren't looking for pity, it's just that holidays are a very poignant reminder that their loved one is gone. What used to feel like a happy celebration may no longer feel that way. Consider sending a card on holidays that say something like, "Thinking of you today and sending love."

# How To Talk
# To a Sad Cat

# Listen, Be Present, Be a Witness

One of the greatest gifts you can give a Sad Cat is to just listen. Listening without trying to fix someone can be very challenging because we often equate giving advice with helping. Likewise, tolerating silence can also be really difficult because we're not used to it; we often rush to fill it with nervous talking.

When you're with a Sad Cat who is really distraught, it's good to give them the floor and just let them cry or vent or even laugh—whatever comes up for them. Your job is to listen, not to fix their grief or make them feel better.

If you feel uncomfortable, just breathe and feel your feet on the floor. Think of your role as a witness who is holding space for them to process their grief. You don't need to say anything except maybe an occasional:

- "I'm sorry."

- "This is heartbreaking."

- "It's not fair that you lost your loved one."

You don't need to say something at every pause. Mostly just be quiet and present.

If they apologize for being emotional you could say, "It's okay, I can handle it."

# Don't Press for Personal Details

It's human nature to be curious about the details of someone's death, but it's not appropriate to probe for this information, particularly if you're not in someone's inner circle. Pressing for personal details around a death can make you seem like a creepy voyeur digging for gossip. It's not your business. If a Sad Cat wants to share details, they will.

# Own it if You Say the "Wrong" Thing

Sometimes we say something insensitive. It happens. Each Sad Cat will respond differently. Some Sad Cats will let it slide, while some will hiss and instantly turn the moment awkward and uncomfortable. In those instances, instead of getting defensive or collapsing in shame, try diffusing the situation by saying something like:

- "I'm sorry, that was insensitive of me.
  I wasn't thinking."

- "I messed up and said the wrong thing.
  I'll be more sensitive."

- "You're absolutely right. I didn't mean to hurt you.
  I'm sorry."

Most Sad Cats will appreciate that you mean well and that this is new territory for you.

# Don't Make the
# Sad Cat Comfort You

The Sad Cat is not the only one grieving the loss of their loved one. It's likely many others are, too. Sad Cats appreciate that others are grieving the loss of their loved one and may find it therapeutic to have a good cry along with a close friend. It only becomes problematic when the balance tips and the Sad Cat is put in a position of having to comfort others (especially people who weren't particularly close to them or their loved one).

Be mindful of requiring a Sad Cat to expend emotional energy they don't have to comfort you. Right now it's all about the Sad Cat and what they need.

# Say Their Loved One's Name

People often worry that if they say the name of the person who died it will make the Sad Cat cry. It's actually more distressing to a Sad Cat if they feel they can't say their loved one's name without making everyone else in the room uncomfortable. It makes them feel as if their loved one has been erased. Saying their departed loved one's name and recalling memories can be very helpful for processing grief.

Generally speaking, Sad Cats appreciate an opportunity to reminisce and share stories about their loved one. Sad Cats are also usually very appreciative when you share photos you have of their loved one.

# Avoid Platitudes

People often feel as if they need to say something wise and insightful to Sad Cats to help them feel better. This often comes in the form of platitudes. Unfortunately, these trite phrases are not helpful. If you don't know what to say to a Sad Cat, that's okay. You don't have to say anything profound. It's better to say something honest from the heart such as:

- "I don't know what to say, but I'm sad for you."

- "I don't know what to say but I've been thinking about you and hoping you're okay even though I know you're not okay."

- "I don't know what to say, I'm just so sorry."

Most Sad Cats will appreciate that you're trying your best.

# Be Patient with Brain Fog

Brain fog is real. It's a direct result of trauma and can make it difficult for Sad Cats to think. Grieving takes a tremendous amount of energy and Sad Cats are exhausted.

It can be frustrating to others when Sad Cats are having a hard time tracking things, recalling details, or repeating themselves a lot. Be patient with them. If you are exasperated with a Sad Cat, they will feel it. Remember, they are not doing it on purpose!

# Don't Talk About Their "New Normal"

It's best not to talk about a Sad Cat's "new normal." To a Sad Cat, there is nothing normal about the nightmare they've found themselves in. They have to learn how to live the rest of their lives in intense emotional pain that doesn't really get better with time but that they just develop more strength to bear. Referring to this as a "new normal" can feel like trivializing their trauma.

# Be Mindful of
# Grief Comparisons

People have a natural impulse to want to relate to what some-one else is going through. But it's important to appreciate that, unless you've lost the same relation—a child or a partner, for exam-ple—it's impossible to know what their loss feels like. It's not that you can never make any comparisons to your own grief experiences; rather, it's how you frame it.

Try to compose your message sensitively, in a way that doesn't dimin-ish the magnitude of the Sad Cat's loss. You might preface your com-parison with: "I know it's not the same as what you're going through, but when I lost my _____ I felt...."

*Note:* Losing a pet can be utterly heartbreaking, especially if it's the most significant loss you've ever experienced. However, equating it to a Sad Cat's loss of a child or life partner isn't going to make them feel comforted; it will likely have the opposite effect.

# Don't Give Unsolicited Advice

People have the best of intentions, but they often confuse giving advice with being helpful. Giving unsolicited advice is *never* helpful, but it is particularly unhelpful to a Sad Cat. Grief is not a problem you can solve.

Our society tends to pathologize grief and want to fix it. But grief is normal and natural and will take its own, unique course. Nothing—absolutely nothing—you say will help a Sad Cat to "get over it." Unless they explicitly ask for your advice, it's better not to offer it.

# Don't Share Your Own Trauma with a Sad Cat

Sometimes people share traumatic experiences, in a general "misery loves company" kind of way. Unfortunately, this can add to the Sad Cat's distress.

Particularly in the early days of loss, when a Sad Cat is anguished and in shock, they might not have the emotional bandwidth to process anyone else's trauma. It's better to resist any impulse to unload devastating stories onto a Sad Cat, because they may not be able to handle it.

This is a time when it's 100% about the Sad Cat and 0% about you. This will change over time, but right now it's all about them.

# Never Say "Look
on the Bright Side..."

Never say anything to a Sad Cat that begins with either "look on the bright side..." or "at least…" Every Sad Cat would gladly forfeit any "benefit" they've gained from the death of their loved one to see them again, even for a moment. There is no benefit or bright side that makes their pain and agony worth it.

# Be Sensitive About Sharing Dreams

Some Sad Cats dream of their loved one. Some don't, but really wish they would. It can be very upsetting to a Sad Cat when someone tells them they dreamed of their loved one when they haven't dreamed of them yet.

If you want to share a dream about a Sad Cat's loved one, proceed with sensitivity. Start by asking the Sad Cat if they have had any dreams about their loved one.

- If they say *no* (they haven't dreamed of their loved one), don't share your dream.

- If they say *yes* (and if it feels right), say, "I had a dream about them, too. Would you like to hear it?"

  – If they say *no*, respect that and say, "I understand, no problem."

  – If they say *yes*, then share the dream, with sensitivity, taking your cues from the Sad Cat.

# Give Feedback Gently

If a Sad Cat decides to do something impulsive that you think is a bad idea, be gentle with your feedback. Don't tell them they're doing something they'll regret. Instead, encourage them to give it some time and decide later. You could mention that it's generally recommended that Sad Cats wait one year before making any major decisions (recognizing that that is not always possible). If your Sad Cat wants to do it anyway, let it go and love them regardless.

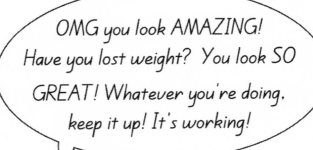

# Don't Gush over How
# Good a Sad Cat Looks

Some Sad Cats lose weight after the death of their loved one because they cannot eat. Their stomach is in knots from the devastation, shock, and loss, and they have no appetite. It's important to understand that it may not be a compliment for Sad Cats to hear that they look great when their weight loss has come at such an agonizingly high price.

# How To Navigate
# Social Occasions

# Be Patient with Social Invitations

No one likes to keep extending invitations to someone when their answer is always no. It's natural to give up after a while. But keep in mind that some (not all) Sad Cats find themselves in a really difficult place of *not wanting to be alone but not wanting company*. It's a terrible, lonely place.

It can be a real kindness to persevere and keep checking in with the Sad Cat (as feels appropriate) until they are ready to reconnect. You might try organizing a "friend tree" where each person takes a turn checking in with the Sad Cat every so often, so it's not left up to one person.

# Anticipate Potential Triggers

When a Sad Cat is up for doing something with you, having some sensitivity around the activity can go a long way. Try to anticipate things that may be upsetting to a Sad Cat. For example, if you invite a Sad Cat to watch a TV show or go to a movie, consider the plot. Does someone die in the movie? Is there a 911 call? Try to find out ahead of time about any potential triggers. If there are some, tell the Sad Cat about it and let them decide if they still want to watch it.

# Greet a Sad Cat
# Even if You're Nervous

Some people panic when they see a Sad Cat. They don't know what to say so they hide or quickly head in the opposite direction. Sad Cats may notice acquaintances and even close friends duck behind an aisle at the grocery store or avoid them at a party. It hurts to feel like people are avoiding you, that your presence makes them uncomfortable.

If you happen to run into a Sad Cat, be ready to say something like:

- "Hi. I've been thinking about you. I was so sorry to hear about your _____ [parent/partner/child]. "

- "It's so good to see you. I've been meaning to drop you a note. I'm so sorry about your loss. "

- "Hi, I feel kind of awkward because I don't know what to say to you, but I'm really sorry for your loss."

Then take your cues from them. Let it be okay for the interaction to feel awkward. It can be brief—you don't need to get into a long conversation.

# Don't Put the
# Sad Cat on the Spot

Don't presume that a Sad Cat wants to talk about their grief and trauma in a social setting, particularly in front of casual acquaintances or strangers. If you're in a Sad Cat's inner circle, you won't have to ask them how they're doing at a social event because you will already know. If you're not in a Sad Cat's inner circle, they probably don't want to "go there" with you, especially not in a group setting. If you run into a Sad Cat at a social gathering, just treat them as you would normally.

# How To Be Respectful On Social Media

## Social Media Post:

Someone i barely know
just died an hour ago
and i doubt their
family even knows bc it
JUST HAPPENED 😳 i feel
so bad for the family
esp if they didn't know
about it before i did 😢
#binxisdead #deathsucks

# Don't Announce a Death on Social Media

In this day and age, with the fast and furious grapevine that is social media, there is no such thing as privacy. However, there is still such a thing as respect. Unfortunately, in the race to get the most attention, respect seems to have fallen by the wayside.

- If you learn about a death (especially before loved ones have been notified), **do *not* share the news.**

- If you have filmed at an accident site where a death occurred, **do not post the footage**.

- When someone dies **do *not* post anything about it on social media** unless you have specific instructions from the Sad Cat to do so.

- If you see an ambulance at someone's house, **do not post about it on neighborhood apps** speculating about what happened.

Put yourself in the Sad Cat's shoes and think about how you would like to be treated if you were in that situation. Have healthy, respectful boundaries around their privacy and their feelings.

Looked at social media at work. Didn't expect to see a photo of their loved one.

# Be Considerate
# With Social Media Posts

t's an act of kindness to consider the Sad Cat's feelings when posting photos of their loved one on social media. Of course, you
aren't prohibited from expressing your own grief over the loss, and
it doesn't mean you have to refrain from ever posting images of the
Sad Cat's loved one. But it is good to consider that it could be distressing to a Sad Cat scrolling through social media to suddenly see
photos of their loved one when they weren't expecting to.

Consider your relationship to the Sad Cat. If you are a remote
acquaintance or an ex-partner, it may not be appropriate to post
photos of the Sad Cat's loved one. If you are a close friend or rela-
tive, you may want to check in with the Sad Cat and let them know
you will be posting photos.

HORRIFIED

# Never Meddle with a Deceased Person's Social Media Accounts

Some social media accounts allow you to "memorialize" the account, which can freeze the ability to post to it. No one should interfere with a deceased person's social media accounts unless specifically asked to do so by the Sad Cat. If you feel an account should be closed or memorialized you could let the Sad Cat know and leave it at that. Do not contact any social media platforms on behalf of the deceased person on your own.

# How To Support
# Someone Who Lost
# Their Partner

Treating myself☺

Yum! Good for you!

# Offer to Be a Texting Buddy

S ad Cats who lose their partner often lose their texting buddy—someone to whom they can text simple things throughout their day, such as a selfie, a beautiful sunset, or a funny video. Depending on how close you are to the Sad Cat, you could offer to be their texting buddy. You wouldn't even necessarily need to say "I'll be your texting buddy." You could just naturally encourage it over time by initiating texts and texting back.

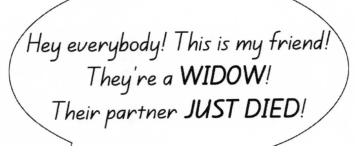

# Don't Introduce a Sad Cat
# as a Widow or Widower

When you're introducing a Sad Cat to people, don't announce that they are a widow or widower. It's not your story to tell. It's not your news. Let the Sad Cat tell people if and when they choose. Just introduce a Sad Cat the same way you would introduce anyone else.

Super fun Friday game night!

Wasn't invited

# Accommodate Changes in Couples Dynamics

I t can be challenging to adapt to a new dynamic when a Sad Cat and their partner were previously part of couples' social get-togethers.

Being a third wheel is a stark reminder that their loved one is gone. On the other hand, it can be even more painful when Sad Cats aren't invited to activities they enjoyed doing with other couples. Single Sad Cats are *very* aware when couples don't want them around—they can feel that their presence is a grim reminder that anyone could be in the Sad Cat's shoes someday.

If you were in a couple's group with a Sad Cat and their partner, ask the Sad Cat how they feel about spending time with couples. If they are fine with it, continue inviting them. If they are uncomfortable with it, find new ways to get together that don't require a partner.

Binx and I only got two years.

# Appreciate that Weddings Can Be Challenging

Weddings (and other happy family occasions) can be challenging for Sad Cats because they are now there as a single person, without their partner at their side. For Sad Cats, weddings are a mix of contrasting emotions: they simultaneously feel happy for the new couple and grief for what they have lost.

Sometimes people assume that a Sad Cat wouldn't want to attend a wedding and believe they are doing them a kindness by not inviting them. It's better to invite the Sad Cat and let them decide if they are up for it. It can also be a kindness to include a +1 on the invitation so the Sad Cat can bring someone along.

If a Sad Cat is in your wedding party and they have recently lost their partner, have a conversation with them ahead of time to find out if they are still up for it. Be extra understanding and supportive of whatever your Sad Cat needs.

# Offer to Be an Emergency Contact

Sometimes a widowed Sad Cat doesn't have anyone to list as an emergency contact. It can be really upsetting for a Sad Cat to go to a doctor's office and have to cross off their partner's name as their emergency contact and not have anyone to replace them with. Depending on how close you are to the Sad Cat, you could offer to be that person.

Made it back from
kayaking ☺

Great! Glad you had
a good time.

# Offer to Be a Check-in Contact

When on an outdoor adventure, traveling alone, or on a date, it's a good safety practice to let someone know where you are and when you have made it home safely. Sad Cats may not have anyone to fill that role now that their partner is gone, so you could offer that. It may be greatly appreciated.

# Don't Say You're a Golf Widow

Don't make jokes about being a widow when your partner is away from home. This isn't to imply that you have to carefully watch every word you say to a Sad Cat, but this one in particular can be difficult for a Sad Cat to hear. Your partner will come home. The Sad Cat's partner will never, ever come home, and when you make a joke about being a widow it trivializes their reality.

# Be Mindful When Complaining About Your Partner

I t can be difficult for Sad Cats to listen to people complain about minor annoying things their partners do, like leaving the toilet seat up or not loading the dishwasher the right way. When a loved one dies it profoundly changes one's perspective about what really matters in life.

This is actually an important lesson to all of us to spend more time being grateful instead of complaining, to appreciate what we have, and not sweat the small stuff. The reality is we never know when we could lose someone we love.

Welcome home, did
you have a good
flight?

Yes, thanks!

# Offer to Pick the Sad Cat Up at the Airport

For widowed Sad Cats who travel, it can be a really difficult moment when the plane lands and everyone else takes out their phone to text their loved ones that they've arrived. It's also heartbreaking for Sad Cats to arrive back home and not have their partner there to welcome them.

You could help by offering to pick your Sad Cat up at the airport, or by making a note of when they will return and text them when they land asking, "Did you make it back okay? How are you doing?"

Check out my new tat, in honor of my ex who just died. We only dated for a summer in high school but Binx was the love of my life!

HORRIFIED

# If You're an Ex,
# Stay in the Background

The passing of an ex-partner can be difficult because all of the attention is on the current partner, the Sad Cat. There typically isn't any space for, or acknowledgment of, your prior relationship to the deceased or the grief you may be feeling. If you're an ex-partner it's important to accept this, as challenging as it may be, and be respectful of the Sad Cat. Be mindful of how and where you express your grief. It may be most appropriate to reserve your grief expressions for your own close friends—not at the celebration of life, the gravesite, or on social media.

Met a kind and supportive person and had forgotten what it felt like to laugh. Navigating complex feelings about grief & dating.

# Don't Begrudge a Sad Cat Who Starts Dating

Sometimes people can be really judgmental about how long a Sad Cat should wait before dating. Some think the Sad Cat should hurry up and start dating before they're actually ready. Others get snarky if they think the Sad Cat didn't wait long enough and is disrespecting the memory of their partner.

The bottom line is, it's no one's business but the Sad Cat's if and when they choose to date. When a Sad Cat gets involved in a new relationship, don't assume they've moved on and aren't grieving their loved one anymore. On the contrary, it can bring up very challenging, complicated feelings. So just be kind and supportive. Everyone deserves love and happiness in whatever measure they can find it.

# How To Support Sad Kittens And Their Parents

# Keep Your Spiritual
# Beliefs to Yourself

When someone dies, people often contemplate the meaning of life and death on a deeper level and want to offer their spiritual beliefs to comfort the Sad Cat and their Sad Kittens. It's important to step outside yourself and appreciate that not everyone shares your religious or spiritual beliefs. You might feel like you're sharing something profound that really helped you, but doing so may actually be inappropriate.

It's especially important not to impose your religious or spiritual beliefs onto Sad Kittens. Always check with the Sad Cat first to find out how they are framing it for their child, and go with that.

# Offer to Spend
# Time with Sad Kittens

Spending time with a Sad Kitten can be really important. It shows them that there are other adults who will help them get through this. You don't have to do anything big—take a Sad Kitten out to eat or get a haircut. If it feels appropriate, invite them for a sleepover or even on your own family vacation.

Don't feel rejected if the Sad Kitten is not open to your invitation—just making the gesture can be very meaningful. If you are already a significant person in a Sad Kitten's life, continue to make yourself even more available.

# Don't Force a Sad Kitten to Talk

I t can be hard for some children to express themselves in ordinary situations, and it's even more difficult when they're confused and distraught. While talking can be very helpful for processing grief, it's important to take your cues from the Sad Kitten. If they seem receptive, you could open the door by saying, "I'm happy to listen if there's anything you want to tell me about your (person)." If they want to talk about the loss, great, just listen without giving advice. If they don't want to go there, be prepared to talk about other things.

# Give Stuffed Animals

There's something wonderfully comforting about stuffed animals, physically and emotionally. Giving a stuffed animal, especially to a younger Sad Kitten, can be a great help. They offer companionship without expecting anything in return. Stuffed animals aren't complicated—you love them and they love you back.

This is also appropriate for adults.

# Fill Gaps Left by
# the Departed Parent

When a parent dies, there are often gaps relating to things the departed parent would have done with or for the Sad Kitten, or things the Sad Cat doesn't have time for. For example, learning how to cook, how to tie a tie properly, how to shave, or talking about menstruation. Some of these things can be awkward or sensitive for the Sad Kitten. Work with the Sad Cat and take your cues from them about how you can best support their Sad Kitten.

"Here's a little something for you to celebrate parent's day with your kittens."

Sends gift card for dinner

# Support a Sad Cat on Mother's Day or Father's Day

Mother's Day or Father's Day can be very difficult for Sad Cats who've lost partners because the partner isn't there to initiate a celebration for them—to help their children make breakfast or buy flowers. You could acknowledge the day by sending a card, flowers, or a gift card for the family to go out for dinner. Or you might ask the Sad Kittens directly how they'd like to celebrate the day and then help make it happen.

# Dad's Day at School

# Be an Ally for Parent's Day at School

M om Day" or "Dad Day" at school can be really difficult for Sad Kittens. Consider being an ally to a Sad Kitten by checking with school administrators and advocating for renaming the day parent's day (or something even more generic to acknowledge parents that doesn't alienate anyone, including all nontraditional families).

# Be Mindful of How
# You Talk About the Death

With Sad Kittens, it's especially important to pay attention to how you frame their loved one's passing. Avoid saying anything that sounds like their loved one is being permanently erased from their life. Instead of saying they don't have a mother/father/sibling anymore or that their loved one is "gone," use a softer word, such as "passed."

# Continuing Support As Time Goes On

# Don't Expect a Sad Cat to Have Their Future Worked Out

Sad Cats' minds, bodies, nervous systems, cells, and entire world have been shattered. Especially in the early days following the death of their loved one, Sad Cats don't know how they're going to get through the next moment, hour, or day, let alone what they're going to do in the future. It's better not to ask what they are going to do next.

Also, be considerate of what is actually your business—your curiosity about what they're going to do next in life may be none of your business, particularly if you're not in their inner circle of friends or family.

# Don't Expect a Sad Cat to Have Energy for Anything Extra

People often assume that a Sad Cat is "back to normal" when they outwardly appear to be doing well. They can be disappointed (or, worse, judgmental) when a Sad Cat isn't willing to take on the things they were up for previously. It's important to appreciate that Sad Cats may have a lot less energy and bandwidth than they did before, especially if they have young children.

Some people take this to an extreme and accuse Sad Cats of "playing the widow card" as an excuse to get out of responsibilities. If a Sad Cat tells you they are feeling too fragile or are too depleted to help out with anything, believe them.

# 1.
## Anniversary of loved one's passing

"Thinking of you and remembering Binx fondly."

# 2.
## Friend sends card

Extra points for getting a card ahead of time and putting a reminder on the calendar to mail it.

# 3.
## Sad Cat feels a little better

# Acknowledge the "Deathaversary"

The anniversary of the day the Sad Cat's loved one died is a big deal for most Sad Cats. Even if the Sad Cat chooses to focus on happier occasions (like their loved one's birthday), the deathaversary can still be a very poignant and painful day. The day leading up to it and the day after it can also be difficult.

If you're a close friend, consider making a note of the day their loved one died and offer to support the Sad Cat on that day, however they would like. Perhaps they would like to do some kind of ritual—ask how they want to mark the occasion. If you're not such a close friend, it would be nice to send a card saying, "Thinking of you on this day."

# Don't Put a Timeline
# on a Sad Cat's Grief

There is no such thing as a grief timeline; linear stages of grief are a myth. A lot of people think in terms of "time heals all wounds" and that the farther a Sad Cat is from the day of their loved one's death, the more "over it" they should be, and able to move on. Unfortunately, it doesn't work this way.

Sad Cats learn how to keep functioning despite feeling crushing grief. Over time, they adapt and become stronger, better able to tolerate the grief. But the grief never actually goes away and can even get more intense over time, as they process more layers of it.

It's a kindness to be patient with a Sad Cat's process and not pressure them to "get over it." Most Sad Cats experience grief in waves—over time they will experience good days and difficult days. It's a gift to have a friend who can hang in there with both.

# Don't Expect the Sad Cat to Bounce Back to Their Old Self

Even though each Sad Cat is unique, all Sad Cats are profoundly changed by their loss. Depending on your relationship to the Sad Cat, this may be more or less obvious. When a Sad Cat is doing something "fun," particularly in the first couple of years after the death of their loved one, they may be struggling in the midst of it. Sad Cats are doing their best to reengage life, but the feeling of enjoyment can be almost a foreign concept.

It's a huge gift to a Sad Cat if you can hang in there while they go through the process of forging a new identity and figuring out who they are now, what they enjoy, and what has meaning in this entirely new and difficult life.

# Understand that the Second Year is Often Harder

Many people assume that Sad Cats are okay and fully "recovered" after a year. Any Sad Cat will tell you that this is not the case—grief does not magically go away after a year. Sad Cats who have experienced profound loss often describe it this way:

- The first year is *surreal:* The Sad Cat is in shock, coping in the midst of a living nightmare that they can't wake from. It's a year of heartbreaking firsts—the first anniversary, birthday, or holiday without their loved one.

- The second year is *real:* The shock has started unwinding and the terrible reality that the Sad Cat will never see their loved one again sets in. They will never hear their voice or feel their touch. Their entire life looms ahead of them and it will not include their loved one. It's a devastating feeling.

Continuing to befriend a Sad Cat in the second year and beyond is a great gift.

PTSD from partner dying suddenly 2 weeks ago. Solo parenting 3 traumatized kittens. Ran out of groceries. Couldn't leave them home alone.

# Appreciate that Anyone Could be a Sad Cat

If you see someone on the road driving slowly, or someone having a hard time controlling their kids in a store, or someone weeping in the produce section, or someone doing anything that may slow you down or inconvenience you, know that they could be a Sad Cat. Perhaps they are a Sad Cat who is distraught because they are on their way home from picking up their parent's ashes, or a newly solo parent who hasn't eaten or slept much in weeks, or a Sad Kitten who is missing their dad.

We never know someone's story so it's important to hold as much love and compassion for everyone as we possibly can, in any moment.

# About the Author

Sheila Hoover has a PhD in Adult Education and twenty years of experience analyzing information and making it accessible for audiences in creative and engaging ways. She has also trained and practiced as an end-of-life doula. The content in this book is based on her own research, connections with others who have experienced profound loss, support groups and organizations, and direct experience in the aftermath of losing her husband, parents, and close friends.

Made in United States
Orlando, FL
28 September 2023

37336492R00109